Palaces, Mansions, and Castles

Debbie Gallagher

Smart Apple Media

Smart Apple Media
2140 Howard Drive West
North Mankato, Minnesota 56003

First published in 2007 by
MACMILLAN EDUCATION AUSTRALIA PTY LTD
627 Chapel Street, South Yarra, Australia 3141

Visit our Web site at www.macmillan.com.au or go directly to www.macmillanlibrary.com.au

Associated companies and representatives throughout the world.

Copyright © Debbie Gallagher 2007

Library of Congress Cataloging-in-Publication Data

Gallagher, Debbie, 1969-
    Palaces, mansions, and castles / by Debbie Gallagher.
    p. cm. — (Homes around the world)
    Includes index.
    ISBN 978-1-59920-151-1
    1. Palaces—Juvenile literature. 2. Mansions—Juvenile literature. 3. Castles—Juvenile literature.
    4. Rich people—Juvenile literature. I. Title.

    TH4890.G344 2007
    728.8—dc22

                                                        2007004643

Edited by Angelique Campbell-Muir
Text and cover design by Christine Deering
Page layout by Domenic Lauricella
Photo research by Legend Images
Illustration by Domenic Lauricella

Printed in U.S.

Acknowledgements
The author and the publisher are grateful to the following for permission to reproduce copyright material:

Cover photograph: Mansion in Hollywood, USA © AA World Travel Library/Alamy.

© AA World Travel Library/Alamy, pp. 1, 21; © Arcaid/Alamy, pp. 22, 27; © Tim Graham/Alamy, p. 10; © Coo-ee Picture Library, pp. 7, 24; © Annedave/Dreamstime.com, pp. 6 (top), 9; © Breck/Dreamstime.com, pp. 8, 30 (center left); © Bridgetjones/Dreamstime.com, p. 4; © Brownm39/Dreamstime.com, p. 30 (bottom right); © Darrenbaker/Dreamstime.com, p. 11; © The DW Stock Picture Library, Sydney, p. 15; © Fairfaxphotos/SMH/Quentin Jones, p. 26; © James Aylott/Getty Images, p. 23; © James Aylott/Online USA/Getty Images, pp. 7, 20; © The Imperial Household Agency via Getty Images, p. 14; © Junko Kimura/Getty Images, pp. 6 (center), 13; © iStockphoto.com/Eric Bechtold, p. 30 (top right); © iStockphoto.com/Jacques Croizer, p. 30 (top left); © iStockphoto.com/Cay-Uwe Kulzer, p. 25; © iStockphoto.com/Alexandru Teodorescu, p. 5; © Legendimages, pp. 3, 6, 16, 17, 18, 19; © Mark Moxon, www.moxon.net, p. 30 (bottom left); © Michael Spencer/Saudi Aramco World/PADIA, p. 30 (center right); © Wikipedia, p. 12.

While every care has been taken to trace and acknowledge copyright, the publisher tenders their apologies for any accidental infringement where copyright has proved untraceable. Where the attempt has been unsuccessful, the publisher welcomes information that would redress the situation.

Contents

Glossary words

When a word is printed in **bold**, you can look up its meaning in the glossary on page 31.

Shelter

Everyone needs shelter, as well as food and water, warmth, and protection. Homes around the world provide shelter for people.

This castle is the home of a British duke and his family.

Palaces, mansions, and castles are large homes. They are owned by people, such as **royal families**, celebrities, and business people.

palace

Monaco's royal family lives in this palace.

Palaces, mansions, and castles

Palaces and castles are **traditionally** homes for royal and **noble families**. A mansion is a large home with many rooms.

Windsor Castle is the home of the British royal family.

The Japanese royal family live in Kokyo Imperial Palace.

European chateaus are homes to many noble families.

People who live in palaces, mansions, and castles often use their home for their job. They need large entertaining areas for meetings and activities.

Hollywood mansions are homes to many celebrities.

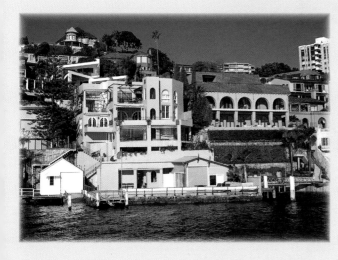

Sydney Harbor mansions are built on the waterfront.

Windsor Castle

Windsor Castle is beside the Thames River near London. It has provided shelter and protection for the British royal family for over 900 years.

High walls protect the people inside the castle.

Windsor Castle has thick walls made from large stones. A **moat** once circled the castle. People had to cross over a **drawbridge** to enter or leave the castle.

castle towers

stone walls

old moat

Windsor Castle's moat is now a garden.

Inside Windsor Castle

There are more than 1,000 rooms inside Windsor Castle. Some rooms are used by the royal family to meet leaders from around the world.

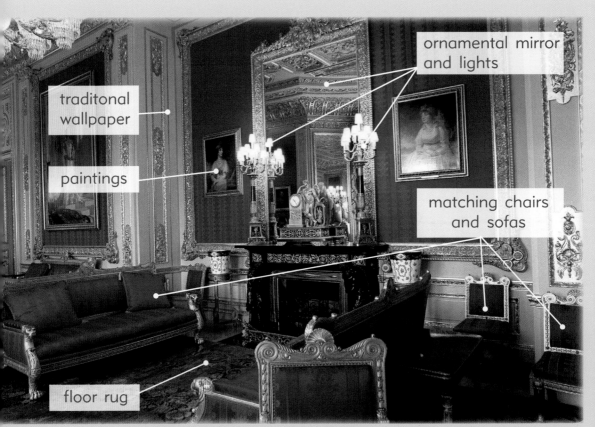

traditonal wallpaper

paintings

ornamental mirror and lights

matching chairs and sofas

floor rug

The Crimson Drawing Room in Windsor Castle has very ornate furnishings.

A large home uses a lot of electricity. Windsor Castle uses **hydroelectric energy** made by the flowing water of the Thames River.

Windsor Castle sits right beside the Thames River.

Kokyo Imperial Palace

Kokyo Imperial Palace has been home to the emperors of Japan for nearly 150 years. It has many buildings and is surrounded by walls and moats.

Kokyo Imperial Palace

Kokyo Imperial Palace is in the center of Japan's capital city, Tokyo.

Kokyo Imperial Palace is built in a traditional Japanese style. The palace has two levels above the ground and one level underground.

The palace has a traditional large, sloping roof.

Inside Kokyo Imperial Palace

Inside Kokyo Imperial Palace are private rooms for the family and public rooms for royal duties. About 1,000 people work at the palace.

wooden floors

Public rooms inside the palace are big and open.

The palace includes many buildings. One traditional job of the Japanese royal family is to raise silkworms. One of the buildings in the palace is called the cocoonery.

There are beautiful gardens and ponds around the palace.

French chateau

Long ago, many European noble families lived in castles. These homes are known by the French word "chateau."

A French chateau may be owned by the same family for hundreds of years.

A French chateau is built with large stone blocks. The stone often came from the nearby area. Sometimes special stone, such as marble, was brought from far away.

tall trees

seating area

formal hedge plants

Many French chateaus have formal gardens like this one.

Inside a French chateau

A French chateau has many rooms. The rooms are decorated with old furniture and paintings. Some have been in the home since it was first built.

old weapons

medals

old weapons

pictures of past family members

old uniform

Things from the family's past are kept in this room.

Because chateaus are large, a family often lives in only one section. Sometimes families grow grapes or give tours to help pay for the care of the chateau.

Visitors pay money for tours of this chateau.

Hollywood mansion

In Hollywood, California, famous people live in mansions. Hollywood mansions are large and have many levels. Some mansions have more than 100 rooms.

There are other buildings on the grounds that are part of the home.

Some Hollywood mansions are built using older, traditional styles. Other mansions look very modern.

several levels

decorative windows

Materials such as brick, steel, and glass are used to build mansions.

Inside a Hollywood mansion

The rooms inside a Hollywood mansion are usually big. Some mansions have a room just for exercising. Some mansions even have a movie theater.

furniture facing view outside

wooden floors

The walls in this high-rise mansion are made of glass.

Most Hollywood mansions have high, strong fences and locked gates for **privacy**. Electronic security systems watch over the home and the grounds.

Many Hollywood mansions have a tennis court and a swimming pool.

Sydney Harbor mansion

Many mansions are built on the hills around Sydney Harbor. The ones at the edge of the water have a dock for a boat.

balcony

large windows

several levels

boat house

private dock

Some Sydney Harbor homes have a dock for the family's boat.

Sydney Harbor mansions are usually made of brick or stone. Most have large windows. Some mansions have more than one level.

Mansions on Sydney Harbor are built to look out over the water.

Inside a Sydney Harbor mansion

Sydney Harbor mansions have many rooms. There are separate cooking and living areas. Sometimes, each bedroom has its own bathroom.

large windows

furnishings

Large windows let plenty of light in this living room.

An outside balcony can be used like another room. There are private gardens around each home.

Balconies look out over the water.

Floor plan

This is the **floor plan** of a castle. It gives you a "bird's-eye view" of the layout of the rooms inside the home.

kitchen

dining room

hallway

laundry

open

hallway

stairs to upper level

records room

entrance

hallway

storage

recreational room

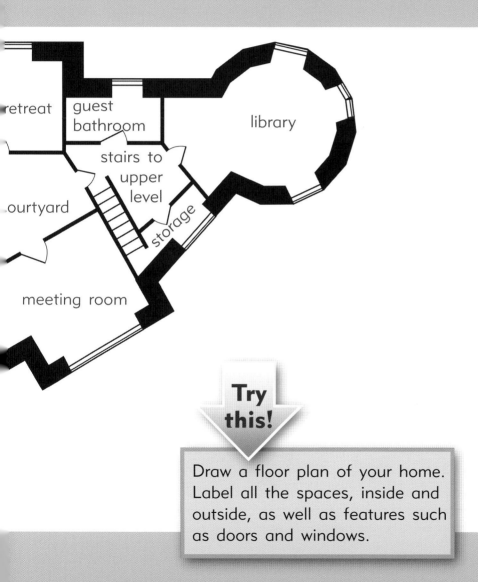

retreat

guest bathroom

library

stairs to upper level

courtyard

storage

meeting room

Try this!

Draw a floor plan of your home. Label all the spaces, inside and outside, as well as features such as doors and windows.

Homes around the world

There are many different types of homes around the world. All homes provide shelter for the people who live in them.

A pit home in Africa

New York City apartments

Windsor Castle in London

Mud and grass homes

Tuareg tent in the
Sahara Desert

Lake home in Asia

Glossary

drawbridge   a bridge that can be lowered over a moat to allow people in and out of a castle

floor plan   a drawing that shows the layout of the areas in a home or building, as if seen from above

hydroelectric energy   power made from moving water

moat   a wide ditch filled with water that surrounds a castle or palace

noble families   families that are part of the ruling class of a country, such as dukes, viscounts, and lords

privacy   being out of public view

royal families   kings, queens, and their families

traditionally   used for a long time by a particular group of people or in a particular area

Index